SEO for Entrepreneurs
2014

By Henrik-Jan van der Pol LL.M.

Version. 2.0

25th July 2014

Table of Contents

Quick Introduction **6**

    What this book covers 6

    Who should read it 6

    How to read this book 6

The Essence of SEO **8**

    Quality is key 8

Setting Everything Up **9**

    Google Analytics 9

    Don't track yourself! 10

    Track events on your website 10

    Google Webmaster Tools 11

    AdWords' Keyword Planner 12

    SeoQuake 12

    Rank Tracking 13

    Collect first data (if you haven't already) 14

    Keep track, measure everything 15

The Status Quo **16**

    SeoQuake 16

        Competitors 17

    Webmaster Tools 17

        Current queries, impressions and clicks 17

        Current links to your site 18

    Google Analytics 19

The 3 Steps of SEO **20**

Focus on What Matters **21**

    Head tail vs. Long tail 21

    How do they find you right now? 21

    Keyword and key phrase research 22

        Google's search suggestions 22

    Ideas from competitors 23

What not matters: an example 24

Analyzing the traffic for possible search queries 25

AdWords' keyword ideas... 27

Get Rid of Ranking Ruiners **28**

Do you have an exact match or keyword stuffed domain? 28

    Exact Match Domains 28

    Keyword stuffed domains 29

Are you suffering from 'old' penalties? 29

    The Way Back Machine 29

    Reconsideration requests 30

Have manual actions been taken? 31

Remove keyword and key phrase stuffing 31

    Measuring your keyword density 32

    Maintaining a natural keyword density 32

Get rid of low quality links to your site 33

    Negative SEO 33

    Analyzing your backlinks 33

    Removing low quality backlinks: the Disavow Tool 34

Remove spammy links 35

    Site-wide links 35

    Footer links.. 35

Fix broken internal links 35

Is your *Above the fold* OK?.. 36

    1024x768 pixels 37

Discard useless categories and tags.. 38

Delete hidden texts 38

Implement Ranking Boosters **39**

Quality content 39

    Choose the right keywords 39

    Offer something extra.. 40

    Use keywords wisely, write naturally 40

Your site's navigation.. 41

Intuitiveness 41

Menu options 41

Search box feature 43

Improve your PageRank: Get valuable backlinks 43

The best way to get backlinks 44

Internal linking 46

Anchor text 47

Increase your Click-Through-Rate 49

Titles on SERPs 49

Meta descriptions 50

Sitelinks 52

Titles, headlines and paragraphs 53

Get social 53

Social media presence 53

Enable social sharing 55

Let visitors interact 55

Contact form 55

Comments feature 56

Consistently use the ALT attribute 57

Submit a sitemap 58

Make sure all pages are indexed 58

Ensure high PageSpeed 60

Exact Match Domains 61

Stay up to date **62**

Recommended Readings **62**

Endnotes **63**

Disclaimer & Terms of Use Agreement

Quick Introduction

What this book covers

This book covers all an entrepreneur needs to know about SEO. Firstly, it helps you set everything up for a good, professional tracking of your website, its traffic and its ranking. Without this, it will be impossible to see what the effects of your SEO efforts are. Secondly, it helps you to focus on the traffic that is valuable to you, to clean up your website and get rid of all the stuff that probably will have a negative impact on your ranking. Then it continues with explaining which techniques you can use to improve your ranking and helps you to understand and satisfy your visitors. After everything is set up properly, you should never stop tweaking and further improving your website, whether these are small improvement or big ones. The book helps you to go through this continuing cycle.

Who should read it

Everyone who quickly wants to learn all there is to SEO and immediately wants to apply the theory in practice. This book enables you to immediately start optimizing your website for search engines. It is called *SEO for Entrepreneurs* because entrepreneurs often lack the time to build up the deep knowledge and skills for the many areas they need to know something about. Whether you will do SEO yourself or will hire someone to do it for you, you always need to have a certain ground level of knowledge.

How to read this book

The book will explain the theory of the essentials, mostly with reference to real-life examples of my own companies. Throughout this book, I will often mention Google while I am talking about search engines. That is because Google today still handles more than two-thirds of global search traffic.

The two companies I will use to bring the theory to life are Perdoo and Aussie.fm. Perdoo (www.perdoo.com) is an online tool for OKR and Todo management. Aussie.fm (www.aussie.fm) is one of my so called automated incomes: an online radio portal for Australians. For both companies SEO has been incredibly important and for both companies we used different strategies and tactics to rank high. I hope it will make reading more fun and help you understand the theory better.

The Essence of SEO

Google's mission, as any other search engine, is to help people find what they are looking for on the internet. Its job therefore is to provide the most relevant search results to any search term.

Search engines like AltaVista and Lycos were very easy to manipulate by using a lot of keywords. When webmasters realized that, many of them started to manipulate the content of their pages. At a certain point, those search engines were therefore not able to generate relevant search results anymore and search never really took off.

When Google started it introduced a search engine which used link popularity to measure the importance of a website. It became harder to work your way up the search ranking if you didn't offer (quality) content that was valued by others and therefore attracted links naturally. Searchers on Google quickly discovered the new search engine was able to generate more relevant results. The result is that it handles two-thirds of all global search traffic today, although the search giant now uses more than 200 factors besides links popularity to gauge relevancy.

Today, Google uses more that 200+ factors to rank its search results (not in the least place due to massive SEO abuse). Links are still important –only nobody really knows how important.

Quality is key

Unsatisfying results might lead Google to changing its algorithm. Since Google receives so many data from its users, it will also know when a user was not happy with a search result. If you for instance google for *second hand automobiles*, click on the #1 result and quickly go back to Google to check out the other results, you probably weren't happy with that first site.

This also means that if you work your way up the SERPs with a lousy website but with great SEO techniques, it will only be a matter of time before Google catches up with you and will prevent your website from ranking high. And once it did, it will be close to impossible to ever regain that wonderful position without dramatically improving your content.

Setting Everything Up

First, we set everything up in order for you to be able to track and measure anything that has to do with the traffic on your website. Not only to map the status quo, but also to see in the future what effects your optimization work will have.

Google Analytics

An important part of SEO is keeping track of your website's traffic to see if your changes have had any effect. Google is constantly tweaking its algorithm so it's very important to keep an eye on it. You probably have a Google Analytics account already but if not, you should immediately get one. Google Analytics is free (although there is also a premium version which will cost you around $150,000/year USD). If you need help to set up your account properties and tracking code, go to http://goo.gl/QSeD67.

Create account

http://google.com/analytics/sign_up.html or http://goo.gl/KIRCQ8

Wordpress

If you have a Wordpress website then download the very simple *Google Analytics* plugin (I have a preference for simple yet effective plugins that just do the job they supposed to do and not much else).

Download

http://wordpress.org/plugins/googleanalytics/ or http://goo.gl/QILRvw

TIP

Using Google Analytics you can later create your own experiments and put yourself into a continuous Tweak-Measure-Learn cycle, which sooner or later will result in a top ranking for your website!

Don't track yourself!

While improving the SEO of your website, chances are you'll be visiting your website yourself pretty often. You don't want your (or your employees') visits to be tracked in Google Analytics.

The *Google Analytics Opt-out Add-on* prevents your data from being used by Google Analytics. Install this add-on in your browser.

This add-on is available for Microsoft Internet Explorer 8-11, Google Chrome, Mozilla Firefox, Apple Safari and Opera.

Download
https://tools.google.com/dlpage/gaoptout or http://goo.gl/2KUAlX

Track events on your website

Google Analytics mainly tracks how a user came to your website, which pages it visited and how much time it spent on each page. If you want to track more user interactions, you need to set up event tracking. Events are a visitor's interactions other than visiting pages within your website. Signups, ad clicks, downloads, video plays, button clicks or scrolling down to a certain section are all examples of actions you can track with Events.

When you should track events

Event tracking becomes really useful if you receive traffic from different sources and want to measure the interactions of visitors from each source separately. For instance, for Perdoo (http://www.perdoo.com) we have a Beta signup form on our landing page. We receive traffic from many different sources. For each individual source we can measure what percentage of visitors converts in a Beta signup. When we started our first AdWords campaign we got a lot of traffic out of it but it didn't result in many Beta signups. Because the conversion rate was much higher for traffic from other sources we knew we were attracting the wrong kind of visitors with our campaign. Since we knew this, we were able to improve our AdWords campaign accordingly and ended paying much less per Beta signup. AdWords is of course not SEO, but you get the point.

How to track events

If you have a Wordpress website, tracking events is rather simple. Download and install the plugin *WP Google Analytics Events*. Watch the short instruction video if you have troubles configuring it.

Download

http://goo.gl/NAN4Ed

Instruction video

http://goo.gl/md3oYQ

If you don't have a Wordpress site it is a lot harder to set up event tracking. It goes beyond the scope of this book to explain this but you will find all the information you need on Google's Support pages: http://goo.gl/JkgHBC.

Google Webmaster Tools

Now that you have everything regarding Google Analytics set up properly, it's time to move on to Google Webmaster Tools. Webmaster Tools is another free program helping you to improve and optimize your website.

As said before, Google Analytics primarily shows you how many hits your site gets, where your traffic is coming from and what content is popular. In other words: Google Analytics gives you all the statistics and data regarding the traffic on your website.

Google Webmaster Tools on the other hand, is Google's way of communicating with you about the performance of your website. If there are issues with your website (like crawl errors or link problems) you will be warned via Webmaster Tools. It also provides you with information regarding your website's performances in search results, obviously crucial to anyone doing SEO! In short: Google's Webmaster Tools helps you create a healthy, Google-friendly site.

Go to https://google.com/webmasters/ to sign in to Webmaster Tools with your Google account. Add your website and verify it (if you have configured Google Analytics properly, just click *Verify* and you shouldn't encounter any problems).

If you want to know more about Webmaster Tools, watch this short video from Google:

http://goo.gl/kggraX

AdWords' Keyword Planner

You normally use AdWords to run Search Engine Advertising (SEA) campaigns, the paid ads that you see on Google's Search Engine Results Pages (SERPs). However, AdWords contains a powerful tool called the *Keyword Planner*. You need an AdWords account to access this tool.

Visit the link below to create your AdWords account. You can use your existing Google account again. If you don't skip the guided signup process, it might seem that Google forces you to directly create your first campaign. You can skip this however.

Create account

http://goo.gl/1OFaKl

After login, click on *Tools* in the menu and then *Keyword planner* to access this tool.

SeoQuake

SeoQuake is a very popular and handy SEO-tool which allows you to see a large number of SEO parameters for any website. It works for Chrome, Firefox, Opera and Safari browsers.

Amongst many other things you will be able to see the PageRank for any website you visit, as well as measure the number of times a certain keyword or phrase appears on that website. It highlights the nofollow links and on SERPs it shows you all these parameter under each result.

It's a powerful tool but it should be handled with care. Frequent use of large amount of parameters may lead to a ban from search engines. If this happens, you need to delete cookies and change proxy server to continue. It may also be that some information is not up-to-date.

Download

http://seoquake.com

Rank Tracking

Tracking your Google (or any other search engine's) ranking is crucial to SEO optimization. Google Webmaster Tools provides you with a lot of valuable information. Go to *Search Traffic - Search Queries*.

Webmaster Tools

Site Dashboard

Site Messages

▸ Search Appearance ⓘ

▾ Search Traffic

　Search Queries

　Links to Your Site

For our radio website, www.aussie.fm, we see that we rank on average 3.5 for the keyword phrase *live fm radio*.

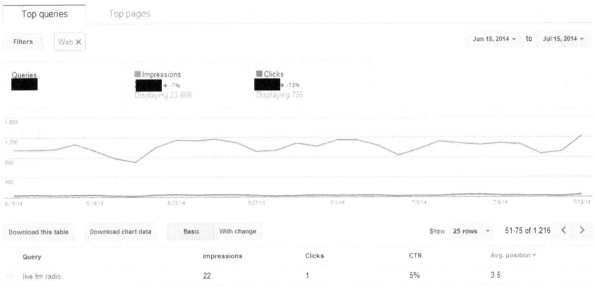

In addition to Webmaster Tools, you need a program like Rank Tracker. Rank Tracker is an easy tool that shows you how your site ranks in Google and Yahoo, but there are many similar tools out there that can do more or less the same.

Download

http://www.link-assistant.com/rank-tracker/ or http://goo.gl/XEvmlO

Important

If someone searches on Google, he sees personalized or local results. The results you see in Webmaster Tools already factored that in. The results you will see via tools like Rank Tracker have <u>not</u> factored in personalized results and might thus give a somewhat skewed impression.

Collect first data (if you haven't already)

If you didn't have Google Analytics already collecting data for your website then first let it track your website for 2-3 weeks. This will help you get an impression of the current traffic on it. Later you can use this data to see if your changes have had effect.

Keep track, measure everything

I really recommend you to keep track of all the SEO changes you make to your website. It's a small effort and it will help you estimate if changes have had the desired effect. I use a simple Excel file for this and as you can see I too am sometimes too lazy to fill in all the details.

	A	B	C	D	E
1	Date	URL	Change	Old	New
2	20-Feb-14	n/a	Launched new site; Added link to Google+ and Twitter		
3	23-Mar-14	aussie.fm	Changed Title, Meta descriptions and Meta keywords		
4	2-Apr-14	n/a	Company added to Google Places		
5	22-May-14	n/a	Google Places verified		
6	18-Jul-14	n/a	Submitted sitemap via Webmaster Tools		
7	18-Jul-14	aussie.fm	Demoted sitelinks Help, Request a station, About us, Mobile, Contact us		
8	23-Jul-14	n/a	Disavowed 2 URLs		
9	23-Jul-14	aussie.fm	Fixed broken link Google+	https://plus.google.com/+Aussie FmAustralianRadio	https://plus.google.com/+Aussie Fm-australia-online-radio

The Status Quo

Before we start we need to capture the current state of your website. It is important to know that some data regarding the current ranking of your website might not be 100% accurate. Unfortunately, sometimes more up-to-date information just isn't available. Nonetheless the data gives you a good first impression and if you haven't made any changes recently, it's probably reliable data.

SeoQuake

Visit your website while you turn the SeoQuake bar in your browser. You don't need all the results from SeoQuake since you will be able to extract some of the information from other sources. Save – at least – the following results in an Excel sheet:

- Google PageRank
- Alexa Rank
- Compete Rank
- Domain age
- Tweets
- Facebook likes
- Google +1s
- Internal/External links

As for Aussie.fm these results are as following (probably hard to see but the results are also listed below):

Important

More about PageRank will follow later in this book. For now it is important to realize that a PageRank applies to individual pages and not your entire website. The same goes sometimes up for Tweets, Facebook likes and Google +1s. You may therefore want to repeat this exercise for every page you want to improve.

Competitors

It's always good to know where you are compared to your competitors. As for Aussie.fm, one of its main competitors is Australia.fm (if you don't know who your competitors are: just Google the search terms that led visitors to your site). Collecting the same information for competitors gives me an impression of how you are performing in relation to them.

I combined the overview for easy comparison.

	A	B	C
1	Date: 16 July 2014		
2			
3		Aussie.fm	Australia.fm
4	Google PageRank	1	4
5	Alexa Rank	14591285	13143260
6	Compete Rank	n/a	n/a
7	Domain age	04-Sep-07	21-Mar-04
8	Tweets	17	0
9	Facebook likes	49	71
10	Google +1s	5	0
11	Internal / External links	73 / 3	54 / 18

As you can see, my competitor has a much higher PageRank.

Webmaster Tools

Log into Google Webmaster Tools to get some additional data for the current status of your site.

Current queries, impressions and clicks

Go to *Search Traffic* and then *Search Queries*. Have a look at in how many search results you currently show up and how many clicks for your site this has generated.

I would recommend you to download the table because Webmaster Tools' history is limited. Save the file in such a way that you can easily see for which timeframe the data is.

Current links to your site

Within *Search Traffic*, go to *Links to Your Site* and have a look at who links to what content on your site (these links are called backlinks). Save the *Total links to Your Site* in the Excel overview with PageRank and other data. For Aussie.fm, the results are:

Subsequently, click on any of the upper two *More*'s and hit *Download latest links*. Save this overview as a CSS, edit the layout a little and then save the file in such a way that you can easily find the status quo of your backlinks for that date.

	A	B
1	Links	First discovered
2	http://wikipediamaze.com/wiki/Timeline_of_Australian_radio	26-06-14
3	http://en.wikipedia.org.advanc.io/wiki/Timeline_of_Australian_radio	24-06-14
4	http://encyclopine.org/en/Timeline_of_Australian_radio	23-06-14
5	http://www.tuugo.biz/m/Companies/aussie.fm/0050001450152	15-06-14
6	http://www.keywordspy.ca/organic/domain.aspx?q=aussie.fm	07-06-14
7	http://www.askives.com/mmm-fm-radio-brisbane.html	07-06-14
8	http://just-like.net/page/news/online-streaming-radio-australia	03-06-14
9	http://en.wikipedia.org/wiki/Timeline_of_Australian_radio	01-06-14
10	http://search.facewap.ru/search.html?q=Listen+to+92.5+GOLD+FM&%E2%88%93site=mobile&uid=1?dc=mgc_home	28-05-14
11	http://www.secretsearchenginelabs.com/find/fm%20106	27-05-14

You can check the backlinks via   Majestic SEO (http://goo.gl/H2vn2K) although this
information tends to be less accurate.

Google Analytics

Of course you should also know the current traffic for your website. Google Analytics though,
provides excellent options to go back in history and compare results. There is thus no need to
save any data.

You now have a good impression of the current status of your website.

It's time to start with SEO!

The 3 Steps of SEO

As said, Google's job is to find the most relevant results to any given search term. They want to help searchers find what they are looking for.

Google found a way to figure out what your website or page is about and how important and relevant it might be to someone performing certain search queries. They will know if someone liked the generated search results because satisfied searchers won't return to Google to check out other results or rephrase their search query. And they can probably also see bounce rates and the time spent on a site.

If you want your site to rank high in Google, you need to know what it is you want to rank high for (unless you're a website like Wikipedia, you will probably not rank high for almost everything). As said, Google will find out if the search results were satisfying. Therefore, trying to rank high for things you don't offer value to a user will never have long lasting effects and might even result in long term negative effects.

Once you figured out what traffic you need, it's time to get rid of all the stuff on your website that has a negative impact on your ranking. When optimizing your website for search engines, Google allows certain techniques called *White Hat SEO*. You should definitely make use of these. However, if you try to mess with the system (*Black Hat SEO*), they may punish you. Have you ever done so in the past, you must clean up this mess first. Once your website is freed from these *Ranking Ruiners*, you should start implementing *Ranking Boosters*.

In short, SEO consists of 3 steps:

1. Focus on What Matters
2. Get Rid of Ranking Ruiners
3. Implement Ranking Boosters

Focus on What Matters

If you don't know where you're going, it is hard to get there. That is also valid for SEO: if you don't know where you want to rank high for in the results pages of search engines, it's quite hard to optimize your site for it. So what visitors do you want to attract to your website?

Not all traffic is the same. Optimizing your website or a specific page for certain traffic (we will talk later about how to do this but keyword stuffing is definitely not part of it) might result in an increase of traffic from that segment but if this segment does not tend to stick around nor interacts with your site, it is probably not of any value to you.

So you need to know what brings in quality traffic. And the first step is to find out what people are searching for. This will also help you get an idea of what content may be valuable to them.

Head tail vs. Long tail
Long tail search terms are specific, nice search phrases. They are usually more than 3 words in length. You can imagine that these search terms offer lower competition and lower search volumes than generic search terms (called *head tail*). However, searchers using long tail queries often have a much better idea what they are looking for and it is very likely that your conversion rate will be higher on this traffic.

For my radio portal www.aussie.fm for instance, we could try to rank #1 for every Australian searching for *radio*. Not only will this be hard to achieve, you can also imagine that a large part of this traffic is not actually looking to listen to the radio via the internet. We would have a much higher conversion on the traffic for a search term like *listen to radio via the internet*, but then these search volumes will be lower.

How do they find you right now?
If you only just launched your website or only just added Google Analytics to your site, you won't have a lot of data.

Have a look at the current queries you show up in, your average position for these queries and the amount of clicks it generated for you site. You already have seen this information, it's located under *Search Traffic - Search Queries* in Webmaster Tools.

Keyword and key phrase research

There are 2 sources for finding out what words and phrases potentially valuable visitors may use in their search queries: Google's search suggestions and Adwords' keyword ideas.

Google's search suggestions

The easiest way to find this out is to put yourself into the shoes of your target audience and start Googling. The best way to do this is to open a new, incognito browser tab and go to the search engine that your target audience will probably use (google.com, google.de, google.co.uk, etc.). In the case of Aussie.fm we use www.google.com.au.

While typing your search query into the input box, Google will automatically show you the most popular related queries.

I can do this for several possible search queries and I will save all these queries, including Google's suggestions in a new Excel file.

	A	B	C	D
1	Source: www.google.com.au			
2				
3	listen to radio online	free radio	listen radio	listen radio online australia
4	listen to radio online free	free radio australia	listen radio online	listen to radio on the internet
5	listen to radio online perth	free radio streaming	listen radio national	listen to radio on the computer
6	listen to radio online nova	free radio online	listen radio live	listen to radio on the web
7	australian radio	streaming radio	listen radio online melbourne	listen to radio on the internet for free
8	online radio	streaming radio australia	live radio	
9	online radio stations	streaming radio stations	live radio streaming	
10	online radio australia	internet radio	live radio australia	
11	online radio streaming			

For all these different searches, I also scroll to the bottom of the first SERP to find more related search queries. Some might be useful, others definitely are not. Again, save all interesting suggestions into your Excel file.

Searches related to **listen to radio on the internet**

how to listen to internet radio on **iphone**
listen to **ham** radio on the internet
listen to **xm** radio on internet
listen to radio **without** internet
listen to internet radio on **android**
how to listen to internet radio on **ipad**
listen to radio **2** on the internet
listen to internet radio on **ps3**

1 2 3 4 5 6 7 8 9 10   Next

Important

You can do this research as extensively as you like. You can repeat the exercises above by starting a search term with 1, 2 or 3 words and then start the next word with a, b, c, etc. and go through the entire alphabet this way.

Important 2

Keep in mind that the shorter the search phrase (head tail) the more difficult it will be to rank high here. You can probably realize a higher conversion on the long tail search phrase (3+ words).

I now have a first impression of how Australians search for websites where they can listen to online radio in general.

Ideas from competitors

Visit your competitors' websites to see what they offer to their visitors. Can you see what keywords and key phrases are important to them? Also look in the source code of their pages for title, meta description and maybe even meta keywords.

What not matters: an example

Of course, a lot of Australians will also Google for a specific radio station to listen to online. I can thus repeat this exercise for every radio station on my website. However, if I google one of the popular radio stations on my website like *ABC Classic FM*, I see that on page 1 of the SERPs for the search phrase *Listen to abc classic fm* there are only links to ABC (and they all have a high PageRank). It will probably be a waste of energy to try to get on the first page for this search term. Being on page 2 will probably not get me any traffic since someone using this search is most likely looking to listen online to this particular radio station and the first hits will serve him perfectly.

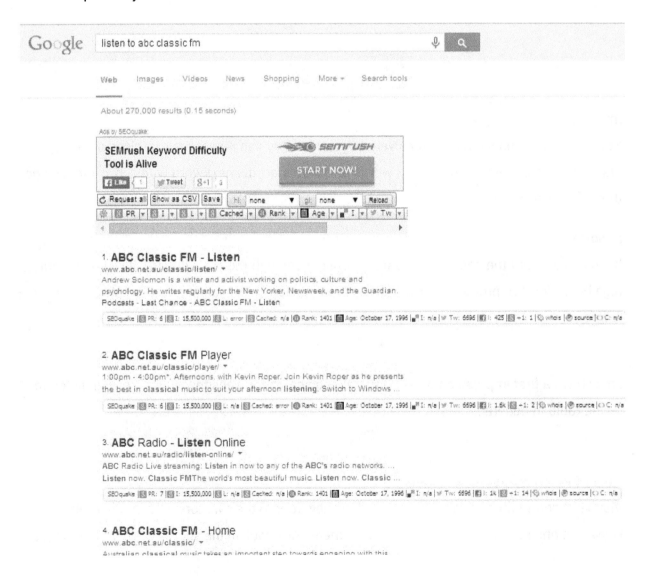

For smaller stations this appears to be <u>not</u> the case.

Analyzing the traffic for possible search queries

The next step is to run all the possible search queries through the AdWords Keyword Planner. As you see in the screenshot I have copy/pasted the terms into the input box but it is probably easier to just upload your Excel file (but you must first save it as a CSV file).

Under Targeting I selected *Australia*. Many keywords and phrases on my list are general terms like *listen to the radio online*. Someone in the United States (google.com) will get different results than someone executing the same search in Australia (google.com.au). I also selected *Google and search partners* instead of just Google.

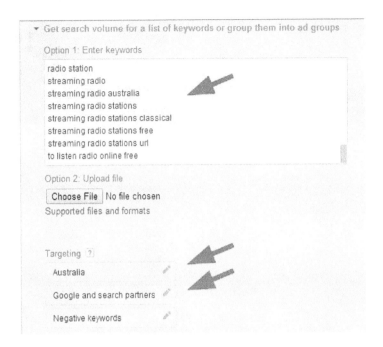

Click on *Get search volume* to see the average monthly searches and competition levels for each term. You now have the opportunity to further narrow your results, for instance by selecting a specific language (a Googler in Australia using a Dutch interface on his computer will get different search results). For Aussie.fm narrowing down for language doesn't make any sense. In the case that Aussie.fm was focused on Dutch radio listeners, than I wouldn't have selected a country under Targeting but I would have selected Dutch as a language. Than I would have gotten the results for worldwide search traffic for everyone using a Dutch interface. Since most people in Australia will have an English interface, like many other countries in the world, this is not possible for Aussie.fm.

Organizing the results

I would advise you to download the results as an Excel file for easier analysis. I personally get out all the columns, except *Ad group, Keyword, Avg. Monthly Searches* and *Competition* (competition tells you how competitive advertising is for each keyword). You can then sort them in several ways to get the desired overview.

	A	B	C	D
1	Ad group	Keyword	Avg. Monthly Searches	Competition
2	Keywords like: Free Music	free music	18100	0.67
3	Radio	internet radio	9900	0.5
4	Radio	online radio	5400	0.14
5	Radio	live radio	1900	0.07
6	Free Radio	free radio	1600	0.25
7	Listen To Radio	listen to radio online	1300	0.21
8	Radio	online radio stations	1300	0.25
9	Radio	australian radio	1000	0.1
10	Radio	internet radio stations	720	0.32
11	Radio	radio station	720	0.24

As you can see *free music* is by far the most popular term, however it is only slightly related to Aussie.fm's content and the competition for it is high. This doesn't necessarily mean it will be hard to rank high for this keyword but in this case it most certainly is.

AdWords' keyword ideas

To get even more ideas go back to AdWords and click on the tab *Keyword Ideas*. Here you will see another (huge list) of ideas Google has for keywords for your website. If you download these it will also contain the list from above. Organize them in the same way to simplify analysis.

You now have an idea of how many people search for search terms related to your website. It is useful to have a good understanding of this.

Get Rid of Ranking Ruiners

I call everything that potentially ruins your ranking, *Ranking Ruiners*. Most Ranking Ruiners are the result of Black Hat SEO activities. You might still benefit from it at this moment, but Google eventually catches up and may demote your site or completely remove it from the SERPs. Better to remove them immediately.

Do you have an exact match or keyword stuffed domain?

Exact Match Domains

An EMD or Exact Match Domain is a domain that uses a keyword phrase as its domain name, e.g. www.pomegranatejuicebenefits.org (for those webmasters targeting pomegranate juice benefits). EMDs aim to rank high by being very 'specialized'.

Since late 2012 the ranking of poor quality EMDs was reduced with a new update of Google's search engine. See Matt Cutts's (who leads Google's Webspam team) announcement on Twitter:

If you have an EMD, there is no reason to panic. This 'algo change' is focused on demoting <u>low quality</u> EMDs. If you have a quality website which happens to be on an exact match domain you are probably safe. However, you risk being scrutinized and it's still advisable to go for a brandable, easy-to-remember domain.

Keyword stuffed domains

There isn't much you can do about keyword stuffed domains. It's better to move your site to a new domain (unless it is ranking well or still generates a welcome income). Keyword stuffed domains like buy-viagra-online-no-prescription.com look spammy and will make visitors wary.

Are you suffering from 'old' penalties?

It can happen than your domain has been penalized by Google before you even owned it. One of the previous owners could for instance have taken part in Black Hat SEO techniques and the domain penalty has been carried on to you. If your domain never ranked properly, this might be the cause.

The Way Back Machine

The Way Back Machine (http://archive.org/web/) allows you to see the history of your domain and what was on it. If I do this for Aussie.fm I get the following results:

INTERNET ARCHIVE
WayBackMachine   http://www.aussie.fm   BROWSE HISTORY

http://www.aussie.fm
Saved **63 times** between September 4, 2007 and July 8, 2014.

PLEASE DONATE TODAY. Your generosity preserves knowledge for future generations. Thank you.

| 1996 | 1997 | 1998 | 1999 | 2000 | 2001 | 2002 | 2003 | 2004 | 2005 | 2006 | 2007 | **2008** | 2009 | 2010 | 2011 | 2012 | 2013 | 2014 |

JAN	**FEB**	**MAR**	**APR**
1 2 3 4 5	1 2	1	1 2 3 4 5
6 7 8 9 10 11 12	3 4 5 6 7 8 9	2 3 4 5 6 7 8	6 7 8 9 **10** 11 12
13 14 15 16 17 18 19	10 11 12 **13** 14 15 16	9 10 11 12 13 14 15	13 14 15 16 17 **18** 19
20 21 22 23 24 25 26	17 18 19 20 21 22 23	16 17 18 19 20 21 22	20 21 22 23 24 25 26
27 28 29 30 31	24 25 26 27 28 29	23 24 25 26 27 28 29	27 28 29 30
		30 31	
MAY	**JUN**	**JUL**	**AUG**
1 2 3	1 2 3 4 5 6 7	1 2 **3** 4 5	1 2

Apparently someone else owned this domain before I did, during 2007-2009. The blue dots indicate snapshots that are taken from the domain at that date. Clicking on one of those snapshots shows me that someone else has had the same idea as I had.

Although this was really fun to discover, it doesn't tell me if my website has been penalized due to 'illicit' optimization by the previous owner. Aussie.fm however ranks pretty well so it is unlikely that I suffer from an old penalty.

Reconsideration requests

If you discover that your domain was used before you and think you may suffer from an old penalty, you could file a *Reconsideration Request* at Google via Webmaster Tools (http://goo.gl/HO246O). If Google can see that the domain has changed hands, you'll have a good chance of being reconsidered.

Have manual actions been taken?

Google recently added *Manual Actions* to its Webmaster Tools. Generally, the search engine relies on algorithms to evaluate and improve search quality. But sometimes manual actions are taken which might result in a demotion or complete removal of your site from the search results. When such actions have been taken you will find them under *Search Traffic - Manual actions*. If you find any actions here, immediately address these problems. Once you're confident your site follows Google's Webmaster Guidelines again you can file a Reconsideration Request (see *Reconsideration Requests* above).

Remove keyword and key phrase stuffing

Google states on its website: *"Keyword stuffing refers to the practice of loading a webpage with keywords or numbers in an attempt to manipulate a site's ranking in Google search results. [...] Filling pages with keywords or numbers results in a negative user experience, and can harm your site's ranking.*[i]*"*.

It then goes on with giving an example: *"We sell custom cigar humidors. Our custom cigar humidors are handmade. If you're thinking of buying a custom cigar humidor, please contact our custom cigar humidor specialists at custom.cigar.humidors@example.com."*.

It is pretty clear for what key phrase this text is trying to rank high for. In a text block of only 29 words the phrase *custom cigar humidors* appears 5 times. That's a keyword density of 17%! As a result, the paragraph is annoying to read and doesn't make sense. Would anyone who not writes for search engines write such a text?

Stuffing your website with keywords and phrases was one of the ways how many webmasters pushed their website up the rankings of Google and other search engines. You probably have seen such sites a few times: when reading it is pretty clear these texts were written for search engines, not visitors. Luckily for web searchers this does not work anymore. Google is able to detect these Black Hat SEO techniques and will punish the website in its ranking, sooner or later.

Does your content sound natural?

Measuring your keyword density

You can measure your own webpage's keyword density using SeoQuake. For Aussie.fm it is as following:

Total number of words: 70				
Keyword	**Found in**	**Repeats**	**Density**	**Prominence**
radio	T, D, K	4	5.71%	57.50%
aussie.fm	T, D, K	3	4.29%	46.67%
listen	T, D	3	4.29%	70.95%
live	T, D, K	2	2.86%	75.71%
australian	T, D, K	2	2.86%	84.29%
station		2	2.86%	79.29%
request		2	2.86%	82.14%

Total 2-word phrases: 5				
Keyword	**Found in**	**Repeats**	**Density**	**Prominence**
fm radio	D, K	2	5.71%	32.86%
to australian	T, D	2	5.71%	84.29%
listen to	T	2	5.71%	85.71%
a station		2	5.71%	79.29%
request a		2	5.71%	80.71%

Total 3-word phrases: 2				
Keyword	**Found in**	**Repeats**	**Density**	**Prominence**
listen to australian	T	2	8.57%	84.29%
request a station		2	8.57%	79.29%

And of course I also looked up the results for my competitor.

Maintaining a natural keyword density

Is repeating the same phrase 17 times every 100 words natural? There isn't a yes or no answer to that. Natural is the keyword density that occurs when someone who is knowledgeable about the subject writes that text (without writing for search engines of course).

Google has several ways of analyzing what your webpage is about, besides looking at keywords. LSI, or Latent Semantic Indexing, is one of them and it's worth reading this article (http://goo.gl/hQVGNm) and watching this video (http://goo.gl/XoNfO3). For now it is enough to know that when you Google for *pomegranate juice benefits*, only THREE of the top 10 search results use that exact phrase on their page (and TWO of them only use this phrase ONCE). Try it yourself and try it for any search term that is not the name of a product or brand name. As you will see, the top 10 results have far fewer pages amongst them containing the exact search term on its page.

So be sure to remove any keyword stuffed articles from your website and make your texts sound natural again. If you are not an expert in the field, Google your competitors and look at the words they use.

Get rid of low quality links to your site

Links to your site (backlinks) are still incredibly important for your page authority, or PageRank. It's why many webmasters in the past have taken part in link schemes, link farms or bought links to their website. It's also why you still see many ads on SEO related websites that try to sell you links or link building tools.

It's important to know that Google does not want you to buy backlinks (or sell links to other sites). If they find out, they will punish your site. Google says: *"Buying or selling links that pass PageRank can dilute the quality of search results. [...] Buying or selling links that pass PageRank is in violation of Google's Webmaster Guidelines and can negatively impact a site's ranking in search results."[ii]*. If you have taken part in link schemes in the past you might have seen your page rank better but you can be sure it won't last. Read the following article if you tend to trivialize this: http://goo.gl/colkkJ.

Negative SEO

When webmasters build low quality links to the sites of their competitors with the sole aim of getting it penalized, this is called negative SEO. It's relatively new but it is most certainly a reality. It seems relatively easy to bring down your competition this way, that's the reason nobody ever expected Google to make this possible.

Analyzing your backlinks

Open the backlink overview which you have created in the chapter *Current Links to Your Site*. Scan your list for any links that you think may harm your site. The list might be long so this can be a tedious thing to do. You will get better at it and after the first link audit you only have to check changes.

You can double check doubtful backlinks by visiting these pages with your SeoQuake bar enabled. You will then also see the PageRank of these pages and as you know, receiving backlinks from pages with a high PR is of more value.

Removing low quality backlinks: the Disavow Tool

If you have found harmful backlinks that you control you should of course remove those yourself. For the backlinks you do not control you can use Google's Disavow Tool.

If you want to remove single URLs with the Disavow Tool, just copy these backlinks to a .txt file. To remove an entire domain you need to type *"Domain:example.com"* into the text file. When you're finished, go to the Disavow Tool (http://goo.gl/Dh8y4z), upload the file and hit *Submit*.

After a while you should see all these links removed from the *Links to Your Site* overview.

Disavow Links

This is an advanced feature and should only be used with caution. If used incorrectly, this feature can potentially harm your site's performance in Google's search results. We recommend that you only disavow backlinks if you believe that there are a considerable number of spammy, artificial, or low-quality links pointing to your site, and if you are confident that the links are causing issues for you.

The file below contains the list of disavowed links. To edit the list, click **Download**.

Disavowed 20140718.txt   Download   Delete

Results for the submission on July 18, 2014 1:32:38 PM UTC+2
You successfully uploaded a disavow links file (Disavowed 20140718.txt) containing 1 domains and 2 URLs.

Choose File

Submit   Done

Important

Be careful with this feature, it can harm your ranking in the search results!

Remove spammy links

Site-wide links

Site-wide links are internal or external links that appear on all the pages of your website. Be careful with those and if it doesn't serve a clear purpose like increasing conversion it is probably best to get rid of them. If you use them, stay away from keywords and keyword phrases you are trying to rank high for as it is a clear violation of Google's guidelines.

Site-wide links generally appear in the header, navigation menu, sidebar or footer. These site-wide links serve a useful purpose: making your website better navigable. Definitely use these but don't make them keyword-focused. Label them so that they are helpful to your visitors.

Footer links

Links in the footer are not a problem, they might be even beneficial. But if you use footer links on your site white the sole aim of making another page rank better for a certain keyword, remove them. Check your site for links with keyword rich anchor texts that don't make a lot of sense besides improving the ranking of that other page.

Fix broken internal links

To check for any broken links on your site there are 2 tools I would recommend: http://www.brokenlinkcheck.com or w3school's tool which you'll find under http://validator.w3.org/checklink. Both of them are free and both of them are good. I tested many others but they missed broken links that these tools both found. I prefer to work with the first one because it's faster and it leaves out results that don't matter, such as 'broken' links due to AdSense ads.

Scan the results for any broken links and correct them.

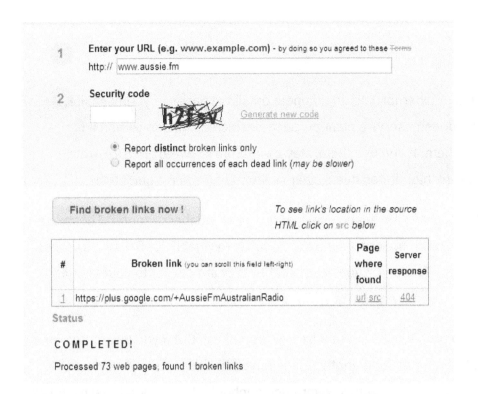

Is your *Above the fold* OK?

Early 2012 Google made a change to its algorithm that looks at the layout of the webpages in its search results and the amount of content you see *above the fold*. *Above the fold* means the viewable area in your browser before you scroll down. As you can read in Google's blog post in which they announced the algo change (http://goo.gl/RuC4Fz), this change is due to many complaints from users that if they click on a search result it is difficult to find the actual content.

Google: *"Rather than scrolling down the page past a slew of ads, users want to see content right away. So sites that don't have much content "above-the-fold" can be affected by this change. If you click on a website and the part of the website you see first either doesn't have a lot of visible content above-the-fold or dedicates a large fraction of the site's initial screen real estate to ads, that's not a very good user experience. Such sites may not rank as highly going forward."*

In the past many webmasters made good money with launching so called AdSense sites. These were over-optimized highly ranking webpages that offered visitors little content besides money-generating ads. Visitors had 3 options: go back to Google, click on an ad or scroll down to find the meager content. As you can imagine (and you probably landed yourself on some of these sites), this is indeed not a good user experience.

1024x768 pixels

According to w3schools, 99% of web users have a screen resolution of 1024x768 pixels or higher[iii]. It is therefore advisable to resize your screen to 1024x768 and check how your pages look like. Is there meaningful content above the fold? If not, change it.

Important

It is ok to have some ads above the fold, as long as it is to a *"normal degree"*.

As you can see, there is not so much difference between Aussie.fm on screen resolution 1366x768 (first) then on 1024x768 (latter). I think my site is doing fine.

1366x768

1024x768

Discard useless categories and tags

Categorizing and tagging is a nice way of organizing the content on your website. However, don't overdo this – especially not when trying to rank higher this way. If you have tags that you only use once or twice, remove them. If you have tags identical to categories, remove them. Don't keyword stuff you categories and tags. Focus instead on increasing the user experience of your site by structuring your content properly.

Delete hidden texts

A popular way to fool search engines was to hide texts on a page. This way users were not bothered and you could still put all the keyword stuffed texts on your site. The simplest way to do this is of course to write in a white font on a white background. Search engines of course catched up and marked this as a Black Hat SEO technique.

Detect hidden texts on your pages by clicking anywhere on a then hit CTRL-A (Windows) or Command A (Mac). This will select everything on that page and allow you to see any texts that may be hidden. Should you find hidden texts, remove them immediately.

Implement Ranking Boosters

Quality content

For content quality, Google provides 2 guidelines:

- *"Could the content appear in a magazine?"*
- *"Is your content the type of content that people will want to bookmark, or share socially?"*

The second question deserves some extra attention since Google most certainly is able to detect bookmarks and social shares. They can therefore include these in their algorithm.

Choose the right keywords

As said before, it doesn't make any sense ranking high for search terms to which your page has not much to offer. By measuring things like time on site and bounce rate, Google has great indicators for how happy a visitor was with the search result. Besides that, the traffic is retty useless to you. Better make sure to rank high for search terms that are a good match to your content.

Niche vocabulary

Having that said, it's important to know that for every search term, there is something like a nice vocabulary. This niche vocabulary are the words and phrases that any expert on the subject would use in his content. Don't regard 'expert' here as a scholar or pundit. By expert I mean anyone deeply involved in that particular subject. If you have an ecommerce site selling women's shoes, the expert's niche vocabulary are the words and phrases the women within your target group would use when talking about these shoes.

If you want to rank high for related search terms, you should use these words and phrases too! Now, if you are an expert on the subject or if you are deeply involved in the matter at hands, this shouldn't be much of a challenge to you. You will probably use these words naturally and that's also the reason why it is best to become an authority in the subject of your site.

However, if you are not an expert or hiring a ghost writer to write your content, you better do good research on the words and phrases to use. How this research can be done is demonstrated in *How Do They Find Your Site Right Now?*. Don't forget to execute relevant searches and see what words the pages use that currently rank high.

Writing content using nice vocabulary might take a little longer to write but it is well worth it. As a bonus you will probably start ranking higher for a bunch of longtail search terms.

Offer something extra

It's hard to find search terms that don't generate many search results already. Does your site offer something extra to the top #10 search results Google already has for your search term? If that isn't the case, why do you think your page should replace one of the current results?

Google used to display messages like "*In order to show you the most relevant results, we have omitted some entries very similar to the 704 already displayed. If you like, you can repeat the search with the omitted results included.*". Although it seems they don't show this message anymore, it is an indicator that Google is looking for unique content for every search term and is less likely to present pages with similar content in the top #10 search results. Instead it is more likely to add content that offers something extra and adds value to the existing top search results.

In order to show you the most relevant results, we have omitted some entries very similar to the 801 already displayed.
If you like, you can repeat the search with the omitted results included.

Of course this goes for each individual search. Google sees only a limited number of pages as relevant for each search phrase.

You can add additional value by adding for instance special images, your own opinion or thoughts on a matter, personal experiences or maybe even a poll.

Use keywords wisely, write naturally

Always write for your target audience, your visitors. _____ If you're writing about a topic you don't know much about, this is probably hard. Where necessary, make sure to gain some insights for the field you are writing about. Learn the nice vocabulary that enables you to write naturally. If you are not sure about the keyword-use in your article, let a friend read it. Can he pick out keywords or key phrases that the article seems to rank for? Do phrases flow naturally?

Forget about keyword density, anyone talking about that is too far behind on SEO. Re-read *Remove Keyword and Key Phrase Stuffing* if that helps. The appropriate keyword density is any degree that flows from content written naturally by an expert. Whether that is 0.1% or 3%.

Of course you can and should use keywords in your texts. But just make sure that what you write is driven by what visitors want instead of keyword research. Content written with the visitor in mind will have a better chance in Google. Think what article or what text a visitor wants to see first, then go and see which keywords are relevant.

Your site's navigation

The better your website's structure, the more likely people will find what they are looking for on your website. Many searchers are very impatient. Unless you offer something unique that a visitor can't get anywhere else, a disorganized, cluttered website will make him press the back button. As discussed, this can have a negative influence on your future ranking. It is therefore important that you help visitors navigate your site.

When creating the navigation, make sure you do it first for the visitors (and not the search engines)!

Intuitiveness

Good website navigation is intuitive. Since you probably spend or have spent a lot of time on your own website, you'll need someone else to test the intuitiveness of your website. Bounce rates and Time on site (see Google Analytics) are also indicators that your website could be improved on this point.

Let a friend browse your website and ask him to look for certain information or product. You will never know if you get honest feedback from friends and family so it is probably best to sit next to him. Watch him clicking through your site. How long does it take him?

Menu options

Generally, there are 4 options to place your site's navigation menus:

1. Header
2. Sidebar
3. Content area
4. Footer

You will probably have certain links that you don't want to put somewhere else than in your footer. The more menus you have and the more links these menus contain, the more cluttered it will become. So building a good navigation for your website is an art in itself. Note again that intuitiveness is crucial. Intuitiveness is one of the reasons why the iPod became an incredible success while so many other MP3 players didn't.

Dynamic navigation

If the number of pages on your website is rather small, a header (or sidebar) and footer menu will suffice. Bigger websites need additional navigation. From a certain amount of pages it makes sense to make the navigation page depended. You shouldn't do this for the menus in your header and footer because it will confuse visitors. The best place for dynamic navigation is the content area or sidebar. You'll probably have seen this on a number of pages you visited in the past.

Imagine for instance that own a travel website and a visitor is looking at a review from a restaurant in Amsterdam. It would probably be most useful to the visitor if that page offered him links to other articles about Amsterdam or The Netherlands, for instance information about hotels and things to do there. As you can see, this won't really work on smaller websites, but is really useful on bigger ones!

A note for Wordpress users

If you have a Wordpress-based site, creating a dynamic navigation is simple. As with many features you want on your Wordpress site, there are plugins for it. Two of them are worth mentioning.

- **Dynamic Widgets**: a sidebar menu is a widget and this plugin allows you to define on which pages which sidebar should appear.
- **Yet Another Related Posts Plugin (YARPP)**: this plugin allows you to show links to other content on your site, relevant to the post a visitor is currently at. These links to other related content is displayed at the end of each post. This is also directly beneficial to

your search engine ranking since it improves your internal linking by linking related content together.

Many people dislike spending time searching for specific information on a site and hit straight for the search box. A search box will also help those that spend some time scanning your pages but couldn't find what they were looking for. Since adding a search box nowadays is so simple, I would highly recommend you to do so. Especially if your site grows bigger and bigger. If you're not yet convinced, watch this video from Google: http://goo.gl/xDFrhd.

The best way to add a search box is via Google Custom Search (http://www.google.com/cse/). The paid version is worth the money.

Wordpress' search box

Wordpress has a default search box but its performance is often poor. There are some search plugins for Wordpress and they probably function better than the default. Perform a few searches yourself to see if it generates the results as you like them. Otherwise use Google's Custom Search (and of course there is a plugin to help you with that: http://goo.gl/ad8HnN).

Improve your PageRank: Get valuable backlinks

PageRank is one of the algorithms Google's uses to rank pages in their search results. It's a way of measuring the importance of websites. It works by counting the number and quality of links to a certain page. Every link from page X to page A is considered a vote for page A. If many sites link to A, A becomes more popular and its PageRank will increase, <u>unless</u> A has taken part in a link scheme (manipulating the number of links to your website, for instance via buying links). Google hates link schemes and will punish a site for it.

The PR of A is not only depended on the number of links to A, the popularity (or PageRank) of any website linking to A is also taken into consideration. Your PR will be much higher if just a few pages with a high PR rank to your page, than if many websites with PR 0 or 1 'vote' for you.

The underlying assumption is that more important websites are likely to receive more links from other (quality) websites. Links are only one of the 200+ factors Google uses to rank websites but it was the basis of the earliest version of it search engine and still the most important one. It is based on the cite index of academic papers and was the start of the Google search engine in the first place. PageRank runs from 0 (lowest) to 10 (highest).

Having a high PageRank doesn't guarantee a high placement in the search results (again, PR is just one of the 200+ 'signals' Google uses to rank sites). The opposite is also true, ranking really well doesn't necessarily mean you have a high PR. A study (in 2010) by SEOmoz[iv] illustrates this nicely. By using the Spearman correlation they were able to demonstrate that the correlation between PageRank and a Google's top #10 search result was 0.18 (whereas a score of 1.00 would indicate a perfect correlation and 0.00 would say it's non-existent).

PR on Different Engines

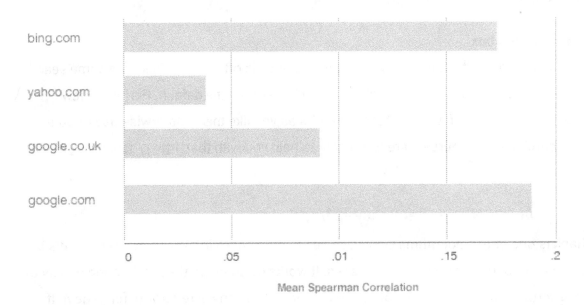

Mean Spearman Correlation

Of course, webmasters only care about PageRank to attract more organic traffic from Google and the only proof of this is given to you by Google Analytics.

The best way to get backlinks

The best way to attract valuable backlinks is still to publish quality content. And by quality, I mean content that your visitors will love and would like to bookmark and share with others. Content, that other webmaster will want to link to. It might take time but it will produce the best long term results.

For Perdoo for instance, we created a few presentations about OKR on SlideShare (http://goo.gl/jEzIJ3). These presentations attracted thousands of views within their first two weeks, resulted in a lot of shared on LinkedIn and generated a lot of links to our website (www.perdoo.com). Within a short time we ranked already very high for OKR related search terms without any content on our site, besides a Beta signup form. The result was a lot of traffic and an incredible amount of beta signups.

Ideas:

- Presentations
  - *Share them for free on platforms like SlideShare (http://slideshare.net).*
- Infographics
  - *Share them on your website and all your social channels.*
- Free downloads
  - *This can be handouts (PDFs) of your presentations, or any content useful to your target audience. Anything you can give away for free in the form of a download helps your link getting shared.*
- 'Lists'
  - *People love lists, and love to share them! If you have a list with for instance the 'Top 10 restaurants in Berlin', make sure to notify the owners of these restaurants that they made it to your top 10. They will probably put a link to your article on their website, to show their visitors how good their restaurant is.*
- Guest blogs
  - *There are many websites and blogs out there, and many of them are constantly on the lookout for new content. Find websites and blogs in your niche and check if you can submit an article which is both relevant to you as well adds value to their site. You can also try to find those sites by googling '"write for us" + keyword'. Where keyword is of course any keyword relevant to your site.*
  - *TIP: if you enable the SeoQuake bar for the search results, you can pick out the guest blogs with the highest PageRank (and as you know links from pages with a high PR are more valuable).*
- Videos
  - *Every person has his own way of 'consuming' content. It is less difficult than you think to create a video from one of your existing presentations. Either stand for the camera or use a voiceover. Share those videos on YouTube (create your own channel), Vimeo, etc.*

Don't forget to include a link to your site in your profile and the video description. If you want to know more about ranking high on YouTube, read my book How to Boost Your YouTube Videos.

And a bonus idea, although this one is slightly different:

- Forums
  - *Or any other feature on your website that allows your target audience to connect with and talk to each other.*

TIP

Browse websites like Quora (http://quora.com) or Yahoo Answers (http://answers.yahoo.com) and see if there are any questions your content might answer.

Important

PageRank applies to individual pages and <u>not</u> to the entire website.

Important 2

While working to improve your PageRank (PR), it might take some time before Google publishes PageRank updates. Although PRs are updated at Google very often, it publishes updates to the outside world only a few (probably 3 to 5) times a year. The reason for this is that Google does not want you to get obsessed about it (and rather focus on providing value). So it's important for you to realize that your PR is being updated but that it will take a while before changes are visible in any PageRank checker like SeoQuake.

Important 3

Also see *Anchor text.*

Internal linking

Internal links are good for 2 reasons. It helps the search engines to crawl all of your pages and it helps you visitors to find other related content on your website. It will thus help to get all your pages indexed and increate the time a visitor spends on your site.

Internal links are common and you see them a lot on websites like Wikipedia. All the blue texts in the Wikipedia article below are internal links.

Internal link

From Wikipedia, the free encyclopedia

An **internal link** is a type of hyperlink on a webpage. Links are considered either "external" or "internal" depending on their target. Generally, a link to a page outside the same domain is considered external, whereas one that points at another section of the same webpage or to another page of the same website or domain is considered internal.[1]

However, these definitions become clouded when the same organization operates multiple domains functioning as a single web experience, e.g. when a secure commerce website is used for purchasing things displayed on a non-secure website. In these cases, links that are "external" by the above definition can conceivably classified as "internal" for some purposes.

One way to improve your internal linking is to use dynamic navigation, as discussed above under *Menu options*. Another important way of internal linking is the method Wikipedia practices as in the screenshot above. In this article they write about internal linking and they link certain words to Wikipedia pages that explain what the corresponding word is all about. So if you read this article and you don't know what a *domain* is, alls you have to do is click on domain and you are taken to the page which explains it. You just hit the back button if you want to continue reading about internal linking. This way of linking is said to have dramatically increased the amount of time an average visitor spends on Wikipedia. More importantly: this type of internal linking will also increase the ranking of the other pages on your website!

Important

Also see *Anchor text*.

Anchor text

The anchor text is the clickable text in a link. It will mostly be blue and sometimes underlined. In this snippet from an SEO article from Wikipedia, all the blue text is a clickable link to the corresponding Wikipedia articles. All the blue texts are the anchor texts.

Search engine optimization (**SEO**) is the process of affecting the visibility of a website or a web page in a search engine's "natural" or un-paid ("organic") search results. In general, the earlier (or higher ranked on the search results page), and more frequently a site appears in the search results list, the more visitors it will receive from the search engine's users. SEO may target different kinds of search, including image search, local search, video search, academic search,[1] news search and industry-specific vertical search engines.

Search engines use anchor texts to help define what the linked-to page is about. So in the example above, the anchor text *image search* will tell Google that the linked-to page is about image search and therefore for what search term this linked-to page may be relevant. That makes sense, right? Apparently, the writer of the article thinks that Wikipedia's article on image search is relevant for this term and links to it.

If many sites seem to think that a certain webpage is relevant for a given set of terms, that page may well manage to rank high if someone searches for these terms, even though these terms do <u>not</u> appear on the page itself!

Nonetheless, anchor texts are not as important anymore as they used to be. Google pays less attention nowadays to the anchor texts of your inbound links and more attention to the topic of the source page. So if you have an article about internal linking and the inbound link's page topic is about SEO, that link would be a valuable one.

Use anchor texts wisely

Because many webmasters abused anchor texts and stuffed them with keywords to rank higher for those keywords, Google has put anchor texts under scrutiny. If a site has too many inbound links that use the exact same anchor text, it becomes suspicious. All these inbound links may not have been acquired naturally. So be careful with anchor texts and don't try to manipulate the system! Google writes on its website:

> Links with optimized anchor text in articles or press releases distributed on other sites. For example:
> *There are many wedding rings on the market. If you want to have a wedding, you will have to pick the best ring. You will also need to buy flowers and a wedding dress.*

However, anchor texts are still a important part of linking. If obtained naturally, you probably don't have a lot of influence on the anchor texts. For the anchor texts you do have influence on and for the anchor texts of the internal links on your site, it makes sense to spend some time thinking about them and make sure you use a variety of anchor texts instead of using the same keyword or key phrase every time.

Importance of the first anchor text

Research by Moz[v] indicates that if a page has two links which are both targeting the same URL, only the anchor text of the first link is used by Google. The anchor text of the second link is completely neglected.

Important

People are lazy and tend to use the page title as an anchor text. You may benefit from this if your page title includes the right keywords.

Increase your Click-Through-Rate

Ranking high in the search results is one thing, but if no one click on your link it is pretty useless. To make searcher click on you and not one of the many other results, you should have a compelling title and meta description in place.

Titles on SERPs

The title of your page will show up as the blue text in the SERPs that contains the link to your page. Without a title they will use some texts they find on the page, which might not be beneficial to you. In addition, titles show up in the tabs of a browser.

Google used to use keywords in titles and headlines as a ranking booster. As with many former ranking boosters, these have been abused by many webmasters. Nowadays, it will definitely not work (in the long term) if you keyword stuff your title. In fact, you'll probably get penalized for it. Write titles and headlines that will encourage a visitor to click on your link!

However, some experiments[vi] by SEOs indicate it still is important that you have relevant keywords in your title. The closer a keyword is to the front of the title tag, the more it will help you improve your ranking and CTR. The best format would be:

Primary Keyword - Secondary Keyword | Brand Name

but be sure to create a compelling sentence out of it which encourages a searcher to click.

To maximize the CTR for your titles, it is good to know that search engines bold keywords in the title when they match the search query.

The title is placed between the <head></head> tags:

<title>This is your title</title>

Aussie.fm: Listen to Australian live radio on the internet
www.aussie.fm/ ▾
Listen live to Australian radio on the internet! More than 65 free streaming fm radio
stations. Aussie.fm - Australia's 1st online radio portal.

Radio Adelaide - Listen to Australian live radio on the internet
www.aussie.fm/Adelaide ▾
Listen online to Radio Adelaide 101.5 fm.

Radio Fremantle - Listen to Australian live radio on the internet
www.aussie.fm/Fremantle ▾
Listen online to Radio Fremantle 107.9 FM.

Wordpress

For Wordpress there are many SEO plugins that make it simpler for you to set your titles and meta descriptions (see below). They often also show you a snippet preview, this allows you to check how that particular page will be displayed on the SERPs. Just Google for *Wordpress meta description plugin*.

HOWEVER, be careful with Wordpress SEO plugins since they often use - or encourage you to use – outdated SEO techniques.

Important

Keep your titles shorter than 55 characters. That way you can be sure your titles are being displayed properly in 95% of the search results. If it's more your risk being cut off.

Important 2

Each title should be unique.

Meta descriptions

Meta description are not a Google ranking factor but they are crucial to making users click on your page and not one of the dozens or thousands other results. The meta description is your opportunity as a webmaster to advertize your content to the searcher and tell him what your content is about. Furthermore, social sites like Facebook and Twitter also use the description when the page is shared on their sites. Without a meta description Google, Facebook and Twitter will use the first texts they find on the page which might not be beneficial to you.

When writing meta descriptions for your pages it is important to write a short, compelling paragraph that reflects the content of that page. Since searchers will also scan meta descriptions for keywords of the things they are looking for, you should make use of them.

Aussie.fm: Listen to Australian live radio on the internet
www.aussie.fm/ ▾
Listen live to Australian radio on the internet! More than 65 free streaming fm radio stations. **Aussie**.fm - Australia's 1st online radio portal.
2GB 873AM - Help - Mix 106.5 - ABC Grandstand

As with titles, it is good to know that search engines bold keywords in the description when they match the search query. In the example below I googled for *Listen to Australian radio*. Also note that Google also bolded *Aussie* although this was not part of my search query. Apparently Google considers *aussie* a synonym for *australian*, or at least considers those two to be highly related.

Aussie.fm: **Listen to Australian** live **radio** on the internet
www.**aussie**.fm/ ▾
Listen live to **Australian radio** on the internet! More than 65 free streaming fm **radio** stations. **Aussie**.fm - Australia's 1st online **radio** portal.

You add meta tags by adding the following to your source code within the <head></head> tags: <meta name="description" content="description of the applicable page">. In Wordpress many SEO plugins can help you to set the meta description for each page.

Important

Make sure the meta description is no longer than 150-160 characters. If it's more it will be cut off on the SERPs.

Important 2

Just as with titles, each meta description should be unique.

Important 3

If you use quotes in your meta descriptions, use single instead of double quotes. To prevent descriptions from becoming too long, Google cuts off quotations. If you use single quotes it won't recognize it as such.

Important 4

Other search engines may still use meta descriptions as a ranking factor!

Sitelinks

The links displayed below some of the search results in Google are called sitelinks. In the screenshot below, these are *2GB 873AM*, *Help*, *Mix 106.5*, etc. Besides *Help* these are all radio stations and that is perfectly fine. I'm not so happy with the *Help* sitelink, because I think it might negatively influence my CTR since people are looking for Australian radio stations. Also, this link is actually a popup on my site and if you click on this link in the search result you only see a white page with the text instead of the Aussie.fm website.

Aussie.fm: Listen to Australian live radio on the internet
www.aussie.fm/ ▾
Listen live to Australian radio on the internet! More than 65 free streaming fm radio
stations. Aussie.fm - Australia's 1st online radio portal.
2GB 873AM - Help - Mix 106.5 - ABC Grandstand

If you see a sitelink below your search results which you don't like, you can ask Google to stop displaying these in the search results. In Webmaster Tools, go to *Search Appearance – Sitelinks* and fill in the form and click on *DEMOTE*.

Sitelinks

Sitelinks are automatically generated links that may appear under your site's search results Learn more. If you don't want a page to appear as a sitelink, you can demote it. Only site owners and users with full permissions can demote sitelinks.

For this search result: http://www.aussie.fm/ Leave empty when demoting a sitelink for home page

Demote this sitelink URL: http://www.aussie.fm/mobile   DEMOTE

Demotions (5/100)   Show   25 rows ▾   1-5 of 5   <   >
Effective until Oct 16, 2014

Search result ▾   Sitelink

 /   http://www.aussie.fm/about-us   Remove Demotion

 /   http://www.aussie.fm/contact-us   Remove Demotion

 /   http://www.aussie.fm/help   Remove Demotion

Titles, headlines and paragraphs

Titles and headlines are important, whether that is on webpages or in books or magazines. It tells the visitor what the content is about. And that's not only important for improving your CTR in the search results (see *Titles on SERPs* above).

Write titles and headlines that will encourage a visitor to keep on reading. Write for humans and not for search machines! Separating your texts into logical paragraphs will increase the readability of your texts and adding titles and headlines where they make sense will help find visitors what they need on your site. This will make a visitor less likely to hit the back button in his browser (and thus tell Google he wasn't happy with the search result) and more likely to spend more time on your site (and thus increasing your time on site and maybe even decrease your bounce ratio).

Get social

There are many reasons to get social. Shares, likes and +1s first of all directly increase your reach. Social channels like Facebook and LinkedIn can also help create links to your page or website. Furthermore, Google can measure the social activity around a certain page and it definitely plays a factor in its ranking. Google indexes tweets, Google knows how many Facebook likes your content or Facebook page has and of course they track the +1s. It is very likely that they use it in their ranking. So get social!

Social media presence

First of all, you need to have a social presence. Depending on the business you're in, you can decide to start using Twitter, Facebook, Google+, Pinterest, YouTube or LinkedIn. Those are the main top social channels (if you want to know more about the main social channels and their Unique Monthly Visitors, check out this link: http://goo.gl/IUYJu8 and this one: http://goo.gl/GPxDme).

You have set up and configured these channels and pages within a matter of minutes. I know a lot of people will tell you that you should only set those up which you really plan to start using but I would set them all up anyway. For one reason because it is best to have your brand or company name blocked. Once your business grows you will probably get active on more social platforms.

Who?

It is an important question to ask yourself, who should have this social presence. Is it the website (brand/corporate/domain name), the website's author or both? In the case of my company Perdoo I decided with my co-founder to go for a mix and build a social presence around myself, since I knew already a lot about OKR and was a huge fan of it. We thought that it made sense to present the people behind Perdoo as OKR specialists instead of the company itself. Because I was using Facebook just for private and wanted to keep it that way, I built my Google+ profile around OKR and Perdoo. Later we added a LinkedIn, Facebook and Google+ page for the company. Since we both dislike Twitter very much we chose not to do anything with it.

How?

You can use all these channels in several ways but I would advise it to use it mainly for building a following and to communicate with them. Depending on the industry you're in they may appreciate relevant tips & tricks, the latest news in your niche or about your company, new products or posts on your website, special offers, and anything else relevant and potentially interesting to them.

There are many plugins and tools out there that help you automate (parts of) your social updates. New videos you upload to your YouTube channel can for instance automatically be added to your Google+ page or you can send out automated tweets when new content is published on your website. The social media channels frequently add new features which help you with this, but it's also worth having a look at Hootsuite (http://www.hootsuite.com).

Important

Make sure all your social channels are linking to your domain. It will be easier for search engines to find your social channels and what's happening on them.

Important 2

It's crucial not to spam your followers and send out too many 'updates'. If you manage to build a valuable following, this is not only social proof to new customers and visitors, these followers can also easily convert into frequent visitors of your website or place for instance repeat purchases. More important for SEO, social channels with thriving communities can rank very well in Google!

Don't expect your visitors to do a lot of effort to share your content with others. Make it super simple for them by adding sharing buttons for social to every article, post or product on your website. Having quality content on your site and social sharing enabled can dramatically increase your reach and improve your ranking. Every visitor will turn into a possible promoter!

Again, there are many plugins and scripts out there that help you do this. You can also go to the social media sites yourself and look for the instructions and code you need to add the corresponding button to your site.

Wordpress

If you run a Wordpress website, adding these buttons is especially easy. Social media sharing plugins I really like are:

- **Sociable** (http://goo.gl/xHWZI5)
- **Simple Share Buttons Adder** (http://goo.gl/HC6qQn)
- **SocialBox** (http://goo.gl/4BeY0r, This one will cost you a humble $ 6 USD but it's worth it!)

Quickly go to the screenshots to see which plugin you like and which one will fit best into your website. They are all customizable to a certain degree.

Let visitors interact

There are two main ways to let visitors interact with you, as the owner of the website/content. They are both simple and straightforward. One of them is a contact form which, I think, every website should have. The other one is to enable visitors to place comments on your products, articles or posts.

Contact form

I always get suspicious if a website does not have a contact form. There are many scripts or plugins out there that help you add one to your site and you should definitely do so. There is no reason not to have one.

Comments feature

You should think briefly if a comments feature fits your site. For some sites it just doesn't make a lot of sense but if it does, I would definitely recommend you to do is. Again, there are (free) scripts and plugins that help you do this. Wordpress even has it built in.

Many visitors like to filter their own opinion and allowing them to do so will increase their involvement. It is also a factor of social proof when your article has a comment thread below it. Make sure to answer on comments if that makes sense, especially if comments are directed to you. It will show visitors there is a real person behind the site and build trust.

Spam comments

Allowing comments may result in spam on your website. Spam is often easily recognized, especially if it contains a link to another site. Other people (or robots) do this to get backlinks to their own site. This is especially harmful when these comments contain links to lousy, low quality sites (like porn websites) that you do not want to be associated with. Since backlinks are valuable to webmasters, they have become very creative in disguising their spam.

Make comments nofollow

The *nofollow* value was originally suggested to stop spam in comments. Adding this attribute to every outgoing link in your comments section will tell search engines not to follow this link and not to include this link in the target page's ranking calculation. Make sure to make all links in your comments *nofollow*.

Never auto-approve comments

It is best to manually approve every comment. It is less time-consuming than you might think. Only approve comments if you think they are genuine, that the person has read the article, that it will add something to the article and that the person is real.

Add Anti Spam scripts or plugins

I don't know of any scripts that will help you fight spam on your website but Google will probably help you find it. For Wordpress I do know there are some good plugins. Take a look at the Growmap Anti Spambot Plugin (G.A.S.P., http://goo.gl/HZ14Ex).

Fake comments

Many webmasters add fake comments to their site to artificially gain the benefits mentioned above. I would strongly advise you not to do so. Most fake comments are easily recognized as such and will have the opposite effect of what you try to achieve. However, research pointed out that it is hard for a Facebook with zero likes to gain a like. Has the page already been liked it is more likely that new ones will follow. The psychological mechanism behind this will probably also lower the threshold for anyone to place a comment if there are already comments by other people. If done properly, I would therefore allow one fake comment per article.

Comments Reply Notification

To further increase the involvement of the (genuine) people that put comments on your website, it is advisable to give them the opportunity to automatically be notified when someone else replies on their comment. These notifications are of course also sent when you reply to their comment. For Wordpress there is a (free) plugin available for this, which you will find here: http://goo.gl/1Yglp1.

Consistently use the ALT attribute

The ALT attribute is used in HTML to define an alternative text. This text is displayed when the element to which it is applied cannot be rendered. It is also used by so called 'screen reader' software, used for instance by blind people. It is advisable to use the alt attribute for the <img> tag so that people who cannot see the image can still interact with it. Imagine for instance that you have a *Read more* button on your site. Without an alternative text, a visitor using screen reader software is not likely to continue reading.

The alt attribute is also important for SEO. Google - so far - is not able to 'read' images, the alt attribute (and the filename!) are the only ways for Google to figure out what this image is about and include it in its ordinary search results or Google Images' SERPs. It is generally assumed that Google also considers the use of the alt attribute as valuable to a visitor and might therefore reward your website with a higher ranking. Optimize these ALT attributes for the user.

It's easy to find any problems with your ALT texts. Go to http://goo.gl/40LiS5, fill in you domain and click *Go*. You will be presented with a nice overview of any possible problems. Short ALT texts can be more descriptive.

Submit a sitemap

A sitemap helps search engines to crawl and categorize a site. It helps them find content which they may not have found on their own. Creating a sitemap is easy. XML is the most widely accepted sitemap format.

Go to http://www.xml-sitemaps.com to create a XML sitemap for your website. Download the created sitemap as an uncompressed XML file and upload it to your domain.

Then log into Webmaster Tools and go to *Crawl – Sitemaps*. Click on ADD/TEST SITEMAP in the top right corner, fill in the location and click on Submit.

Make sure all pages are indexed

There is no way to force Google to index your pages. Google writes on its site: *"Although we index billions of webpages [...] we don't guarantee that we'll crawl all of the pages of a particular site. Google doesn't crawl all the pages on the web, and we don't index all the pages we crawl."*.

To quickly see the number of pages indexed by Google type "*site: www.yoursite.com*" into the search machine.

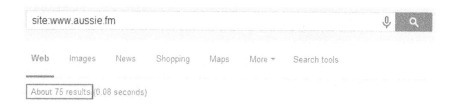

The sitemap, which you should have uploaded by now, will help Google to index all your pages. If you have uploaded your sitemap, you will also see the number of pages within the sitemap. Go back to Webmaster Tools, *Crawl – Sitemaps* and look at the *Submitted* column. Do the numbers correspond?

Now you are in Webmaster Tools, click on *Google Index* and then *Index Status*. Select *Advanced* to see the full status. Here you will also find the total number of pages indexed and spot potential problems (removed pages or pages blocked by robots).

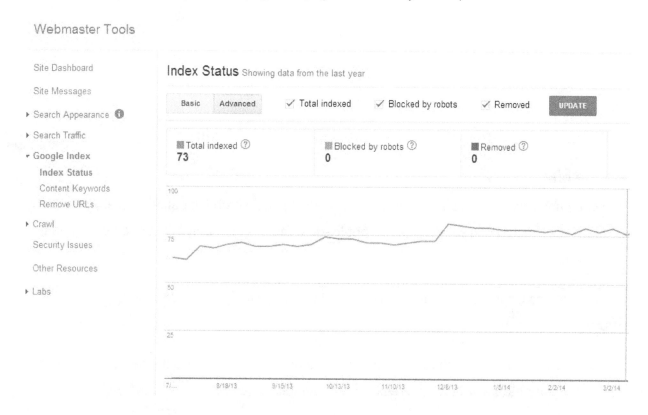

If you see a number bigger than zero under *Blocked by robots* or *Removed*, click on the question mark and *Read more* to solve these problems immediately.

If not all of your pages are index you can request Google to index them (but wait a while if you have only just submitted an up-to-date sitemap. Go back to Webmaster Tools and go to *Crawl – Fetch as Google*. Fill in the URL that is missing from the index and hit *Fetch*. If Google has fetched the URL you can submit it to its index.

Ensure high PageSpeed

You can imagine that it's quite important your website has a high (so called) PageSpeed. Many people are impatient and when a page is not loading fast enough they will just go back and try another result.

It is best to use Google's own tool to get some PageSpeed insights for your site: http://goo.gl/icmLcY

As you can see, for Aussie.fm the results are a reason to worry. I will do the same research for one of my competitors and see his results are much better (81/100).

Luckily, this tool also gives you some ideas on how to fix possible problems. Fix these as soon as possible and – if necessary – move your site to a different server.

Exact Match Domains

If you still need to buy yourself a domain, forget about buying an EMD. You risk being scrutinized by Google which may even result in a penalty. Find a brandable domain name instead, one that is easy to remember. See also *Do you have an Exact Match or Keyword stuffed Domain?* above.

Stay up to date

- http://insidesearch.blogspot.com

Recommended Readings

- *Google Webmaster Guidelines*
  Read here: http://goo.gl/xUJzaL

- *In The Plex: How Google Thinks, Works, and Shapes Our Lives*, Stephen Levy, 2011
  Buy here: http://amzn.to/1zFH8YN

Endnotes

[i] https://support.google.com/webmasters/answer/66358?hl=en

[ii] https://support.google.com/webmasters/answer/93713?hl=en

[iii] http://www.w3schools.com/browsers/browsers_display.asp

[iv] http://moz.com/blog/the-science-of-ranking-correlations

[v] http://moz.com/learn/seo/anchor-text
[vi] http://moz.com/search-ranking-factors

www.ingramcontent.com/pod-product-compliance
Lightning Source LLC
Chambersburg PA
CBHW080604060326

40689CB00021B/4926